Colophon

©Mathias Jansson (2026)

"Promptography: From Light to Language"

ISBN 978-91-86915-89-6

Published by:

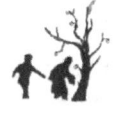 "jag behöver inget förlag"

c/o Mathias Jansson

Tvärvägen 23

232 52 Åkarp

SWEDEN

http://mathiasjansson72.blogspot.se/

Print: Lulu.com

Disclaimer: This book is written with help of ChatGPT. The author has previously conducted extensive research on the subject AI-art and promptography. The texts have been improved, edited and proofread by the author before publishing.

Content

Introduction: Images Written, Not Taken 3

Chapter 1: A Short History of Photography 7

Chapter 2: Art or Reproduction? 13

Chapter 3: From Darkroom to Desktop 18

Chapter 4: Boris Eldagsen – this is not a photo 23

Chapter 5: Defining Promptography 26

Chapter 6: Annika Nordenskiöld -Twin Sisters in Love. 28

Chapter 7: RIVALS – Photography vs. Promptography . 31

Chapter 8: Clint Enns — Plasmatic Bodies 35

Chapter 9: AI.S.A.M — Synthetic Physicalities 40

Chapter 10: Emi Kusano — Techno-Animism 45

Chapter 11: Phillip Toledano's — Another America 50

Chapter 12: Museums Reimagining the Past 55

Chapter 13: Creating Your First Promptography 60

Introduction: Images Written, Not Taken

For a long time, photographs felt simple. You pointed a camera at something, pressed a button, and an image appeared. Whatever the photograph showed—beautiful or ugly, staged or spontaneous—it carried a quiet promise: this existed. Someone stood there. Something happened. Light touched the world and left a mark.

But promptography broke that promise. The images discussed in this book are not taken. They are written. No camera, no lens, no decisive moment. Instead, a sentence is typed into a machine, and an image appears. Often it looks like a photograph: a portrait, a street scene, a historical event, a documentary moment. But none of it ever happened. There was no place, no subject, no past.

This is both fascinating and unsettling. At first glance, promptography feels like a sudden rupture—a radical leap made possible by artificial intelligence. But the shock only feels new because we tend to forget how often image-making has already changed. Photography itself was once accused of being a threat to art. Early critics dismissed photographers as button-pushers, not artists. Later, when digital cameras and Photoshop arrived, many declared the end of "real" photography. If an image could be altered endlessly, how could it still be trusted? And yet, photography survived. Not by staying pure, but by changing.

Promptography pushes this transformation further than ever before. It removes the camera entirely. The artist no longer searches for the right light or the right moment, but for the right words. The creative act shifts from seeing to describing. From framing reality to imagining it.

This raises uncomfortable questions. If images can be generated without any connection to the world, what happens to documentary photography? If portraits no longer need a person, what becomes of identity? And if anyone can create a convincing image of something that never happened, how do we learn to look at images without being fooled?

But promptography is not just about fear or deception. It is also playful, poetic, critical, and deeply connected to older artistic traditions. Long before AI, artists were already creating works through instructions rather than direct craftsmanship. Fluxus artists wrote scores instead of composing music. Sol LeWitt described wall drawings that others executed. In those works, the idea mattered more than the hand.

Promptography continues this tradition—only now, the instructions are carried out by a machine trained on millions of images. The artist becomes a writer. The image becomes a kind of visual sentence.

This book is written for readers who love art but don't necessarily love technical jargon. You don't need to understand how neural networks work. What matters here is how images feel, how they function, and how they reshape our relationship to reality, memory, and imagination.

We will move from the early days of photography to digital images and Photoshop, and from there into the strange world of prompt-generated visuals. Along the way, we'll look at different genres of promptography—documentary, portraiture, landscapes, conceptual works—and at the artists and experiments that define them.

Finally, the book turns practical. Writing prompts is not about mastering a formula. It is about learning how to think visually through language, how to leave space for surprise, and how to collaborate with a system that never quite does what you expect.

Promptography does not mean the end of photography. It means that images have become something else as well: not traces of reality, but proposals. Possibilities. Stories that look real enough to believe in—until we stop and ask how they were made.

And perhaps that is the real challenge of promptography: not learning how to create images, but learning how to read them.

Chapter 1: A Short History of Photography

Long before photographs existed, people already knew the basic trick behind them. In ancient China and Greece, philosophers described the *camera obscura*: a dark room with a small hole that projected an upside-down image of the outside world onto a wall. Artists later used this principle as a drawing aid. The image was there—but it vanished as soon as the light changed. No one could make it stay. The history of photography begins with the desire to stop that image from disappearing.

The First Photograph

In the 1820s, a French inventor named Joseph Nicéphore Niépce managed to do exactly that. Using a metal plate coated with light-sensitive material, he captured what is now considered the world's first permanent photograph: *View from the Window at Le Gras*. The exposure took several hours. The image is faint and grainy, but revolutionary. For the first time, light had been fixed into memory.

Niépce's process was slow and impractical, but it proved something important: images could be made automatically by the world itself.

After Niépce's death, his partner Louis Daguerre refined the idea and introduced the daguerreotype in 1839. The results were astonishingly detailed, but each image was unique—there were no negatives, no copies. A photograph was a singular object, like a mirror that remembered.

The Camera Goes Public

Portrait studios started to appear in cities across Europe and America. For the first time, ordinary people could own images of themselves and their loved ones. This was not just a technical breakthrough—it was a social one. Faces that would once have disappeared into history were now preserved.

Around the same time, William Henry Fox Talbot developed a different approach: the negative-positive process, which allowed photographs to be reproduced. This idea—the photograph as something that could be copied endlessly—would shape modern visual culture more than any single invention.

Cameras slowly became smaller, faster, and more practical. Exposure times dropped from minutes to seconds. Photography moved out of the studio and into the street. The world became photographable.

The First Selfie

One of the most familiar photographic gestures today—the selfie—appeared surprisingly early. In 1839, the American photographer Robert Cornelius took what is widely considered the first photographic self-portrait. He removed the lens cap, ran into the frame, stood still for over a minute, then covered the lens again. It is both awkward and intimate. Even at photography's birth, people turned the camera toward themselves.

Photography Meets Reality

As photography spread across the nineteenth century, it was quickly put to work. Cameras were sent to battlefields, laboratories, distant colonies, police stations, and city streets. Photography became a tool for documentation, classification, and proof. War photography, scientific imaging, ethnographic studies, and criminal records all relied on the camera's apparent neutrality. A photograph did not merely show something—it confirmed it.

By the late nineteenth century, photography had become deeply entangled with ideas of truth, evidence, and memory. To photograph an event was to fix it in history. To photograph a person was to assert their existence. The camera seemed to offer access to reality itself, unfiltered and unquestionable.

One of the most famous examples of this belief came from Eadweard Muybridge. In the 1870s, he was hired to settle a seemingly simple question: did a horse ever lift all four hooves off the ground while galloping? Painters and illustrators had depicted horses for centuries, yet no one knew the answer for sure. Muybridge arranged a series of cameras triggered by tripwires and captured a sequence of photographs that revealed what the human eye could not see.

The images were treated as scientific truth. The camera had revealed reality more accurately than perception itself. Photography was no longer just recording the world—it was correcting it. And yet, even as photography gained this authority, its relationship to reality was never as pure as it appeared.

Photographers staged scenes, retouched faces, and altered bodies. Painted backdrops created imaginary spaces. Multiple negatives were combined into single images. War photographs were rearranged for dramatic effect. Scientific images were selected and framed to support particular conclusions. The camera recorded reality—but reality was carefully arranged.

This contradiction sat at the heart of photography from the very beginning. It was trusted because it was mechanical, yet shaped by human choices at every step. The photograph looked like proof, even when it was persuasion.

That tension—between evidence and construction—would follow photography into the digital age, and eventually prepare the ground for images that no longer needed reality at all.

From Film to Digital

The twentieth century brought color photography, mass-produced cameras, and eventually instant images. When George Eastman introduced the Kodak camera with the slogan *"You press the button, we do the rest,"* photography became something almost anyone could do.

But the biggest shift came at the end of the century, when photography turned digital. Once images became files instead of physical objects, manipulation became effortless. With software like Photoshop, photographs could be altered invisibly. Entire elements could be added or removed. The idea of a "pure" photograph became increasingly hard to defend. And yet, the belief remained.

Even heavily edited photographs were still anchored to something real. A camera had been there. Light had touched a sensor. A moment had occurred. That connection—between the image and the world—survived every technical change. Until now.

Why This History Matters

Promptography arrives at the end of this long story. It looks like photography. It borrows its styles, its genres, its visual language. But it removes the camera—the very thing that once guaranteed a link to reality. There is no exposure, no moment, no original scene.

To understand why this feels so unsettling, we need to remember how deeply photography trained us to trust images. For nearly two hundred years, cameras taught us to believe that images come from the world.

Chapter 2: Art or Reproduction?

When photography first appeared, it was not welcomed as art. In fact, many people thought the idea was ridiculous. How could something made by a machine belong in the same category as painting or sculpture? Where was the skill, the imagination, the human touch? If anyone could press a button and get an image, what exactly was the artist doing?

These questions followed photography for decades. Painters, in particular, felt threatened. For centuries, they had been the official image-makers of society. Now a device could do in seconds what had once taken weeks. Portrait painters lost commissions. Architectural drawing became unnecessary. Some critics predicted that photography would destroy art altogether.

Others dismissed it entirely. Photography, they argued, was not creative—it was merely reproductive. The camera did not invent anything. It simply copied what was already there. And in a way, they were right.

Photography depended on the world. A photograph could not exist without something standing in front of the lens. Unlike a painting, it could not imagine freely. Or so it seemed.

The Fight to Be Taken Seriously

Early photographers were painfully aware of this criticism. Many of them wanted photography to be more than a technical curiosity or a commercial service. They wanted it to be recognized as an art form.

One strategy was imitation. In the late nineteenth century, photographers associated with Pictorialism deliberately made their images look less photographic. They used soft focus, dramatic lighting, heavy retouching, and painterly compositions. Their photographs resembled drawings, etchings, or Romantic paintings. The goal was clear: if photography looked like art, it might be accepted as art. It worked—partially.

Photographs began appearing in exhibitions and salons. Museums started to pay attention. But critics still argued that photography was borrowing legitimacy rather than earning it. It was pretending to be something else.

A New Confidence

In the early twentieth century, a new generation of photographers rejected this approach. Instead of hiding the camera's qualities, they embraced them. Sharp focus, clear detail, and precise composition became virtues rather than flaws. Photographers like Alfred Stieglitz, Paul Strand, and later Edward Weston argued that photography should be valued for what it does best—not for how closely it resembles painting. This was a turning point.

Photography began to define its own aesthetic. The camera was no longer an imitation tool but a way of seeing the world differently. Cropping, perspective, timing, and framing became creative decisions. The photographer's eye mattered as much as the machine. Gradually, photography entered museums—not as documentation, but as art.

Truth, Trust, and the Photograph

Even as photography gained artistic recognition, its reputation for truth remained intact. In newspapers, courts, science, and politics, photographs functioned as evidence. They showed "what happened." The phrase *"the camera doesn't lie"* became a cultural cliché. But the lie was always there.

Photographs could be staged. Scenes could be arranged. Subjects could be directed. Darkroom techniques allowed photographers to remove blemishes, combine negatives, and alter reality long before digital tools existed. What photography really offered was not truth, but *plausibility*.

Images looked true because they followed the visual logic of reality. They felt trustworthy because they resembled the world we know. And most of the time, we accepted that feeling without question.

The Digital Crack

When digital photography and image-editing software became widespread, something shifted. Manipulation was no longer difficult or visible. Anyone could alter an image without leaving obvious traces. Entire scenes could be fabricated using real photographic fragments. Suddenly, the old contract between image and reality felt fragile.

Photojournalism faced crises of credibility. Fashion photography openly embraced artificial perfection. Advertising images drifted further and further from physical possibility. Still, we continued to read images as photographs—because they looked like photographs. The belief survived even when the evidence weakened.

Why This Debate Returns

The arguments once used against photography are now being repeated almost word for word about promptography.

It's not real art.
The machine does the work.
There's no skill involved.
Anyone can do it.

These objections are familiar because we have heard them before.

What history shows is not that these concerns are wrong, but that they miss something important. Every new image-making technology forces a renegotiation of what creativity means. Photography did not eliminate painting. Digital tools did not end photography. They changed how we understand authorship, intention, and originality.

Promptography enters this lineage with a new provocation. If photography was accused of being too mechanical, promptography is accused of being too linguistic. If photographers once defended their artistic choices behind the camera, promptographers now defend theirs in front of a keyboard.

The question is no longer whether the image reflects reality. The question is who—or what—decides what the image becomes. And that question is far from settled.

Chapter 3: From Darkroom to Desktop

For most of its history, photography was physical. Photographs existed as objects. They were printed on paper, stored in albums, hung on walls, or archived in boxes. Even negatives—fragile strips of film—were tangible things you could hold up to the light. Editing a photograph meant working with chemicals, tools, and time. Changes left traces. Mistakes were hard to hide. The darkroom was a place of patience and restraint.

This physicality mattered. It placed natural limits on what could be done to an image. Manipulation was possible, but it required skill and effort. As a result, most viewers still trusted photographs. Alteration existed, but it felt exceptional. Then the image left the darkroom.

The Digital Turn

When photography became digital in the late twentieth century, images stopped being objects and started being data. A photograph was no longer something developed—it was something saved. Light hit a sensor, was converted into numbers, and stored as a file.

At first, this change seemed minor. Digital cameras simply replaced film. Photographs still showed real people, real places, real moments. But something fundamental had shifted.

Once an image became a file, it could be copied endlessly without degradation. It could be emailed, uploaded, resized, and transformed in seconds. The photograph lost its physical anchor. There was no original—only versions.

Photoshop and the New Normal

If digital cameras changed how photographs were captured, Photoshop changed how they were understood. Released in 1990, Photoshop quickly became a standard tool across industries. What had once required darkroom expertise could now be done with a mouse and a screen. Colors could be corrected, bodies reshaped, skies replaced, objects removed.

At first, the changes were subtle. Dust spots disappeared. Exposure improved. Small imperfections were fixed. Then the edits became bolder.

Fashion photography embraced impossible bodies. Advertising perfected artificial perfection. Political images were retouched, cropped, and reframed. Even documentary photography, once considered sacred territory, was quietly adjusted for clarity and impact.

The question was no longer whether images were edited, but how much.

The Collapse of Innocence

Despite all this, photographs still felt real. We continued to read them as evidence, even when we knew—intellectually—that they could be altered. The visual language of photography remained powerful. Sharp focus, natural lighting, realistic textures: these cues signaled authenticity, whether deserved or not.

Over time, a strange contradiction emerged. We distrusted images in theory, but trusted them in practice. This tension exploded with the rise of social media. Images circulated faster than context. Filters normalized aesthetic manipulation. Entire identities were built on carefully curated visuals. Photography became performative, aspirational, and increasingly detached from everyday reality.

Still, the camera remained central. No matter how edited a photograph was, something had been photographed. A body stood there. A place existed. A moment occurred. That connection held the system together.

The Last Step Before Promptography

By the time artificial intelligence entered the image-making process, photography was already halfway abstracted. The image had become flexible, fluid, and negotiable. Trust had shifted from origin to appearance. What mattered was not where the image came from, but how convincingly it looked like a photograph. This is the crucial moment.

Promptography does not arrive in a world of innocent images. It arrives in a culture already trained to accept manipulation, simulation, and aesthetic realism. The leap from edited photograph to generated image is smaller than it seems. Once images became files, the camera stopped being essential.

A Silent Change

What makes this transition so powerful is how quietly it happened. There was no single moment when photography ended. No clear break between "real" and "artificial" images. Instead, the image slowly detached itself from the world, one convenience at a time.

Digital photography made images portable. Photoshop made them malleable. Social media made them performative. Promptography simply removes the final requirement. No camera. No moment. No original scene. Just language, probability, and appearance. The darkroom is gone. The desktop remains. And the image is no longer something we take—it is something we ask for.

Chapter 4: Boris Eldagsen – this is not a photo

In 2023, the art and photography world was shaken by one image—not because it was taken with a camera, but because it wasn't. That image was *The Electrician*, created by the German artist Boris Eldagsen, and it sparked one of the first major public debates about AI-generated imagery and artistic legitimacy.

At the same time Boris Eldagsen coined the term "promptography" to describe his AI-generated images and to highlight that they were fundamentally different from traditional photographs.

Boris Eldagsen is a conceptual artist and photographer whose work long explored the psychological and philosophical dimensions of image-making. He studied philosophy, photography, and fine art across Europe and India, and approached visual practice not as depiction but as an inner journey.

When Eldagsen entered *The Electrician* in the Sony World Photography Awards, he did something unusual: he did not disclose that the image was generated with AI. The black-and-white portrait, evoking an aged aesthetic from the early twentieth century, won the creative open category of the competition—the first time, he argued, that an AI image had won such a prestigious international photography prize.

Soon after the announcement, Eldagsen publicly revealed the truth: the image was not a "photograph" in the traditional sense. It had no negative and no exposure; it was generated from text prompts and refined through multiple iterations using AI tools. He refused the award on principle, arguing that AI images and photography should not compete against each other because they are fundamentally different practices. "AI is not photography," he wrote.

The controversy exposed the tensions at the heart of promptography's emergence. For many in the established photography world, AI-generated images raised uncomfortable questions: What counts as a photograph? Should images created without cameras be judged alongside traditional work? Sony's organizers responded by distancing themselves from Eldagsen, saying they could no longer engage in meaningful dialogue with him because of the way the situation unfolded.

For Eldagsen—and many artists experimenting with AI—the episode was not simply a stunt but a provocation intended to start a conversation about evolving artistic categories. He described AI not as a threat to human creativity but as a liberation from material constraints. With AI, he argued, artists are freed from the physical limits of tools and materials, and instead work through language, imagination, and conceptual intent.

Eldagsen's work *Pseudomnesia*—a series whose title refers to "false memory"—fittingly captures what promptography brings to the visual arts: images that feel like memories of worlds that never existed. The debate that followed his Sony submission helped clarify why the term promptography was needed in the first place: to name this new, language-driven form of image creation that borrows photography's aesthetic cues but differs in origin, process, and meaning.

In the years since, Eldagsen's intervention has become a reference point in discussions about AI in art: not because he proved that AI is better than human creativity, but because he forced the art world to confront a question long looming on the horizon: If an image looks like photography but isn't made by a camera, what do we call it—and why does it matter?

Chapter 5: Defining Promptography

Promptography is more than a technical process—it is a new artistic paradigm. To understand it, we need to explore its aesthetics, its methods, and its philosophical implications. What makes an AI-generated image created through text prompts different from photography, painting, or digital illustration? And why does it matter?

What Is Promptography?

Promptography can be defined as the creation of images through text-based instructions interpreted by artificial intelligence. Unlike photography, which relies on capturing light through a lens, promptography relies on language as its primary tool. The artist does not frame a scene with a camera; they compose a sentence, a phrase, or even a paragraph that guides the algorithm toward a desired visual outcome.

This shift from optical to linguistic creation is profound. In photography, the world provides the raw material. In promptography, imagination does. The prompt becomes the lens, shaping the image through descriptive choices, stylistic references, and conceptual cues.

The Role of the Artist

Who is the author of a promptographic image—the human or the machine? This question lies at the heart of debates about all AI art. While the algorithm performs the rendering, the human artist exercises creative control through:

- **Prompt Crafting:** Choosing words, styles, and references to achieve a specific aesthetic.
- **Iteration:** Refining prompts, adjusting parameters, and selecting outputs.
- **Curation:** Deciding which generated image becomes the final artwork.

In this sense, promptography is not passive. It demands linguistic precision, visual literacy, and conceptual clarity. The artist must think like a writer and a designer simultaneously.

Unlike photography, which is bound by physical reality, promptography thrives on impossibility—a city floating in the sky, a portrait painted by an imaginary artist, a landscape from a world that never existed.

Chapter 6: Annika Nordenskiöld -Twin Sisters in Love

While Boris Eldagsen sparked debate by refusing a traditional photography prize for an AI-generated image, other artists embraced the emerging field of AI-based visual creation with energy and creativity. One striking example comes from Sweden: Annika Nordenskiöld, whose work has helped shape how the art world understands promptography.

Nordenskiöld is a Swedish artist who works across media, blending visual practice with imaginative concept and narrative. In 2023 she entered an image titled "Twin Sisters in Love" in the newly established *Prompted Peculiar – International AI Prize* at the Ballarat International Foto Biennale in Australia. Among over 100 submissions from around the world, her work was selected by a jury as the winner of the inaugural prize.

The image itself is a surreal, black-and-white scene showing two women embracing an octopus. It draws on references from art history and cultural symbolism, but its most striking quality is that none of the people, creatures, or places depicted exist in the physical world—they were generated by an AI based on text prompts crafted by Nordenskiöld.

What set *Twin Sisters in Love* apart, according to the Biennale's judges, was not just its aesthetic appeal but the way it crosses art-historical and cultural references while subtly subverting the documentary conventions of photography and visual realism.

Nordenskiöld worked with the AI image-generation tool Midjourney, crafting detailed prompts that guided the system in producing the final image. For her, promptography is not about creating technically "perfect" images, but about exploring the absurd, dreamlike, and unexpected possibilities that arise when language, imagination, and machine interpretation come together. Her images often play with anatomy, composition, and visual logic in ways that traditional photography never could.

Her work from this period was collected in the book *From Nothing*, published in 2023 by Swedish publisher Max Ström. The book presents a series of AI-generated images that evoke historical photographic styles but reveal uncanny twists—like figures with subtly alien anatomy or dreamlike compositions that feel familiar and strange at once.

Annika's approach and her prize at Ballarat reflect a broader shift in how the art world engages with AI-generated imagery. Some institutions and critics remain cautious, debating whether AI images belong in the same category as traditional photography. Others, like the Ballarat International Foto Biennale, have responded by creating specific platforms and awards for generative work, acknowledging that AI-driven art opens new creative possibilities rather than simply copying old ones.

In this sense, Nordenskiöld's success illustrates how promptography has moved from experimentation into the mainstream of contemporary visual culture—challenging old definitions, sparking debate, and inviting us to rethink what an image can be in the age of generative AI.

Chapter 7: RIVALS – Photography vs. Promptography

In March 2025, something unusual happened in the art world: an exhibition was staged not around a single artist or a single theme, but around a question—a question with real urgency in our time. What distinguishes traditional photography from AI-generated imagery when the two can look nearly identical? What can light, lens and film do that algorithms cannot—and what can AI do that no camera ever could?

The answer took shape in Berlin, at the European Month of Photography (EMOP) 2025, where an exhibition titled *RIVALS – Photography vs. Promptography* brought these questions into the public sphere in a dramatic way. The show was curated by Boris Eldagsen, who has been a prominent voice in the conversation about AI-generated art and promptography.

A Dialogue Between Two Mediums

The exhibition opened on March 1, 2025 at Photo Edition Berlin / Galerie Guelman & Unbekannt in Berlin — part of one of Europe's most important photography festivals. What made *RIVALS* exceptional was its structure: it presented 18 traditional photographers alongside 18 AI artists whose work exists at the intersection between algorithmic imagination and visual culture.

Half of the space was dedicated to conventional photography. Opposite this, the exhibition opened a space for promptography – AI-generated images that create new realities rather than simply record them.

At the heart of the show was a striking pair of works that highlighted the central tension between the two practices: one was Boris Eldagsen's AI image *The Electrician* (2022) — a work generated by a text prompt that had famously won a major photography prize before Eldagsen declined the award — and the other was *FLAMINGONE*, a photograph by Miles Astray. Hung side by side, they marked what curator Eldagsen described as the borderland between photography and promptography.

FLAMINGONE is a striking image taken by Canadian photographer Miles Astray during a trip to Aruba in 2022. The photograph depicts a flamingo with its head tucked under its feathers in such a way that it appears almost surreal—an appearance that makes it look otherworldly or generated. The framing and the moment captured give the bird an enigmatic quality, blurring the line between documentary wildlife photography and creative visual surprise.

What makes *F L A M I N G O N E* particularly significant is not just its composition but its role in the contemporary debate about AI-generated images. Astray entered the photograph into the AI-generated image category of the 1839 Awards (a photography competition focused on creative image work), purposely submitting a real photograph in a category meant for AI works. To the surprise of many, the judges awarded the image third place and also granted it the People's Vote Award—before Astray revealed that it was not AI generated at all.

Astray's intention was to make a statement about how convincingly real photography—and especially unusual or surreal moments captured in the real world—can be mistaken for AI-generated outputs, and conversely how much generative AI has advanced. By submitting a human-made photograph that looks like it could have been created by an AI, he flipped the narrative: instead of AI faking reality, reality was presented as if it could be AI. This twist underscored both the power and the potential confusion of visual technologies in our time.

Because the entry did not meet the competition's rules for the AI category, it was eventually disqualified—but the episode itself became part of the artwork's legacy and its message: humans and nature still produce visual moments that are uniquely alive, unpredictable, and meaningful even in an age dominated by algorithm.

Chapter 8: Clint Enns — Plasmatic Bodies

Some promptographers are interested in beauty, atmosphere, or historical reconstruction. Then there are artists like Clint Enns, whose work makes the uncanny, unsettling, and glitch-like characteristics of AI-generated images a central part of their aesthetic and conceptual appeal. Enns doesn't hide the strange failures of AI — he celebrates them, exploring what happens when machines misinterpret language, bodies, and visual logic.

Who Is Clint Enns?

Clint Enns is a visual artist, writer, and curator with a background in cinema and media studies. His broader practice has long engaged with found footage, glitch aesthetics, and vernacular media, tracing how images travel and mutate in the digital age. With the arrival of generative AI, Enns found a new terrain for his inquiry: not in perfect photorealism, but in where AI fails, slips, and reveals its internal logic.

Enns describes the AI images he's most drawn to as existing between the horrific and the uncanny, following a lineage of found vernacular photography — images that feel familiar because they echo photographic tropes, yet disturb because they never could have been captured in the real world.

Plasmatic Bodies

In his series *"AI Generated Assemblages"* and in exhibitions such as *Plasmatic Bodies* shown at RIVALS: Photography vs. Promptography (EMOP Berlin 2025), Enns displays an astonishing array of AI-generated images whose subjects are hard to categorize: figures with distorted anatomy, human forms that dissolve into other shapes, scenes that feel autobiographical and alien at once.

Titles like *Man Plucking Out His Own Eyes*, *Leggy Minotaur*, *Body Part Incubator* or *Too Many Teeth* evoke the grotesque worlds AI "imagines" when faced with impossible prompts or conceptual contradictions. The images often resemble black-and-white film photography in style — grainy, high-contrast, nostalgic — but their content resists straightforward reading, dwelling instead in the uncanny valley where bodily expectation meets algorithmic bewilderment.

This embrace of the strange places AI stumbles is a deliberate artistic choice. As Enns explained in an interview, he isn't trying to generate polished visuals but rather to highlight where technologies break down or fail. For him, the interest lies not in smoothing over AI's imperfections but in exposing them, letting them shape a visual language that feels both familiar and alien.

From Early AI Tools to Enns' Assemblages

When early text-to-image tools like DALL-E Mini (Craiyon) became widely available, many were fascinated by their glitchy, melting faces and warped forms — artifacts of an imperfect system trying to interpret language statistically rather than visually. These early outputs lacked the polish of modern tools, but their flaws revealed something fundamental about generative systems: they hallucinate.

Enns embraced this effect. Instead of hiding or correcting these misfires, he pushes against them, using prompts that are often self-referential or contradictory, playing the AI against itself to produce images that seem to straddle documentary realism and dream-like distortion. An example described by observers is a prompt like "an AI-generated face" — a kind of meta-commentary on the tool's own process, yielding rows of distorted faces reminiscent of early AI outputs.

While many artists today seek photorealism or narrative coherence from AI, Enns asks a different question: What happens when AI's internal representations of bodies and scenes reveal not a stable reality, but a shifting, collapsed one? In his work, the human form becomes less an anatomical certainty and more an assemblage of intensities, textures, and glitches — a "plasmatic" presence generated as much by algorithmic memory as by prompt intention.

Uncanny Bodies and Visual Culture

What makes Enns' images compelling — and often unsettling — is how they exploit the uncanny valley of AI imagery: figures that look almost human, but not quite, and scenes that feel like documentary fragments from a parallel world. This resonates with broader discussions in promptography about index, authenticity, and artificial realism: while AI outputs often mimic photographic conventions, they reveal their "machine nature" in subtle distortions of anatomy, context, or logic.

In doing so, Enns positions his promptography within a critical lineage: one that recognizes the legacy of glitch art, found footage, and experimental media, while also pushing AI art beyond mere representation into terrain where the errors and hallucinations of the system become expressive material.

Between the Grotesque and the Surreal

Clint Enns' work shows that promptography does not have to chase realism. Instead, it can excavate those moments when the machine's internal logic falters — creating images that are uncanny not because they copy life, but because they expose how life might look when filtered through the machine's dream. Whether these images make us laugh, shudder, or simply pause, they remind us that AI's interpretive errors are themselves a rich source of artistic expression.

In Enns' assemblages, the camera never existed — but the machine's interpretation of photography does, giving us strange echoes of bodies, memories, and images that feel hauntingly familiar yet distinctly unreal.

Chapter 9: AI.S.A.M — Synthetic Physicalities

While much promptography strives toward seamless realism or spectacular fantasy, the work of AI.S.A.M occupies a more ambiguous and productive zone: the space where analogue photographic memory collides with digital generation. His images look as if they belong to the long history of film photography, yet they are entirely synthetic — photographs that never passed through a camera, light, or lens, but still carry the *aura* of photographic experience.

AI.S.A.M's practice is rooted in a deep affection for analogue culture. His *Untitled* series explicitly draws inspiration from lomography, film photography, portrait photography, fashion editorials, and album cover design, recombined through AI tools such as Midjourney, Stable Diffusion, and ComfyUI. The result is what he calls "synthetic physicalities": images that feel tactile, embodied, and photographic, even though they are generated through text and code.

Analogue Aesthetics, Digital Creation

At first glance, AI.S.A.M's images resemble 35mm or 120mm film photographs. There is grain, flash glare, shallow depth of field, and the kind of imperfect lighting associated with on-camera flash photography. Faces are frozen mid-gesture, garments catch the light unevenly, backgrounds fall into darkness. These are visual cues deeply embedded in photographic culture — cues we instinctively trust.

Yet something is always slightly off. The bodies feel too precise or not precise enough. The skin carries a strange smoothness beneath the grain. Expressions hover between emotion and emptiness. The viewer senses that these images belong to photography's visual language, but not to its material reality.

This tension is deliberate. As AI.S.A.M explains, his work explores the intersection between analogue aesthetics and digital creation. Rather than using AI to escape photographic history, he uses it to re-enter that history from an impossible angle, generating images that feel like lost negatives from a parallel archive.

Beauty, Disturbance, and the Editorial Gaze

A key feature of the *Untitled* series is its editorial quality. Many images look like fashion spreads or album artwork: posed figures, strong lighting, graphic compositions. The influence of portrait photography and fashion photography is clear, but stripped of commercial clarity. The images are seductive, but uneasy.

AI.S.A.M describes them as both beautiful and disturbing, familiar and alien at the same time. This duality places his work firmly within the uncanny tradition of promptography, though unlike artists who emphasize anatomical glitches or grotesque distortion, AI.S.A.M's uncanniness is subtle and atmospheric. The disturbance emerges not from obvious errors, but from a feeling that something human has been simulated rather than observed.

The targeted use of flash photography heightens this effect. Flash is historically associated with immediacy, truth, and presence — from crime scenes to snapshots to fashion editorials. By recreating flash lighting synthetically, AI.S.A.M appropriates photography's claim to having been there, while quietly undermining it.

Tools, Control, and Transgression

Technically, AI.S.A.M works across multiple AI systems, carefully shaping outputs rather than relying on a single prompt. This multi-tool approach reflects a broader shift in promptography: from novelty generation toward controlled, authored image-making. The AI becomes a studio, not a gimmick.

Central to his practice is the credo "TRANSGRESSION WITHOUT ABUSE." This statement positions his work ethically within contemporary debates about AI imagery. While pushing boundaries — aesthetic, technological, and conceptual — he explicitly rejects harm to living beings. The bodies in his images may be uncanny, but they are not exploitative; the violence is aesthetic, not physical.

His use of Kodak-inspired colouring and filmic palettes reinforces this ethical and conceptual stance. Rather than treating AI as a break from history, he treats it as a continuation — a way of carrying forward the emotional and visual legacy of analogue photography into a digital present.

Film Is Not Dead — It Has Been Rewritten

AI.S.A.M's work resonates strongly with the mantra "film is not dead." In his case, film survives not as chemistry or celluloid, but as memory, style, and affect. The soul of analogue photography — its imperfections, its intimacy, its sense of physical presence — is translated into a new medium where light never touched a surface, yet the image still feels illuminated.

In the context of this book, AI.S.A.M represents a crucial strand of promptography: one that does not reject photographic tradition, nor merely imitate it, but recomposes it. His images ask us to reconsider what we recognize as photographic truth, and whether the emotional power of a photograph truly depends on its material origin.

In an increasingly digital world, AI.S.A.M's promptographies remind us that beauty, realism, and disturbance are not properties of technology alone — they emerge from how visual language is remembered, reused, and reimagined. The camera may be absent, but photography, it seems, is still very much alive.

Chapter 10: Emi Kusano — Techno-Animism

If promptography is partly about reimagining what photography can be, then Emi Kusano represents one of its most expansive possibilities: the ability to fold cultural memory, speculative futures, and spiritual imagination into a single image. Kusano is a border-crosser by nature — between past and future, analogue nostalgia and digital hyperrealism, pop culture and fine art, technology and myth.

Born in Tokyo in 1990, Kusano grew up immersed in the early digital world: arcade games, anime openings, VHS aesthetics, and the optimistic glow of emerging technologies. These influences remain central to her work, which uses artificial intelligence not as a cold machine, but as a medium for memory, emotion, and belief.

Collective Memory as Promptography

Kusano's AI-generated images transform both collective and individual memories into meticulously detailed visual worlds. Her promptographies often appear hyper-realistic, yet they feel less like photographs of reality and more like photographs of remembered experiences — fragments of childhood, media, and cultural imagination recomposed through AI.

This approach places her work in a distinct position within promptography. Rather than interrogating photographic truth or exploiting AI's errors, Kusano treats AI as a mnemonic device, capable of reconstructing feelings associated with specific eras, places, and aesthetics. The resulting images are emotionally legible even when their subjects are fantastical.

International Recognition and Cultural Reach

Kusano's work has been embraced by both the contemporary art world and the fashion industry — a rare crossover that reflects the accessibility and cultural fluency of her imagery. Her images have appeared as cover art for WWD Japan, been featured in Christie's and Gucci auctions, and exhibited at major institutions including the Saatchi Gallery, the 21st Century Museum of Contemporary Art Kanazawa, and Grand Palais Immersif.

This wide reception underscores a key aspect of Kusano's practice: her work communicates across disciplines. It speaks equally to audiences shaped by anime and pop culture, and to those engaged with contemporary art discourse. AI, in her hands, becomes a universal translator between visual languages.

Techno-Animism: Spirits in the Machine

One of Kusano's central conceptual frameworks is Techno-Animism — the idea that machines, networks, and digital systems possess a kind of spirit or presence. This belief resonates strongly with Japanese cultural traditions, where animism has long shaped how people relate to nature, objects, and the unseen.

In her series *Children's Guardian*, Kusano extends this idea into the realm of promptography. The images depict hybrid beings — part robot, part supernatural — watching over children. These figures evoke the ancient belief that invisible spirits inhabit forests and landscapes, while simultaneously pointing toward a future populated by intelligent machines.

Rather than presenting AI as threatening or alien, Kusano imagines it as protective, gentle, and companionable. The images invite viewers to consider how humans and intelligent systems might coexist in a more harmonious way — not through control or domination, but through mutual presence.

Nostalgia Meets the Future

Kusano's artistic universe extends beyond visual art. She is also the creative force behind Satellite Young, a band that blends 1980s J-pop aesthetics with science-fiction imagery. This fusion mirrors her visual work: nostalgia is not treated as something static or regressive, but as a launchpad for speculative futures.

This sensibility carries directly into her promptography. Her AI images often feel like artifacts from an imagined timeline — futures that remember the past, and pasts that already anticipated the future. The familiarity of anime-inspired characters, combined with AI-driven hyperrealism, creates a visual language that feels emotionally safe yet conceptually ambitious.

Promptography Beyond the Camera

In the context of this book, Emi Kusano represents a form of promptography that moves beyond photography's traditional concerns with index, evidence, and documentation. Her images are not interested in proving that something existed, but in suggesting that something could exist — emotionally, culturally, spiritually.

By merging AI with pop memory, animist belief, and speculative design, Kusano demonstrates how promptography can function as world-building, not just image-making. Her work reminds us that artificial intelligence does not have to erase humanity; it can be used to re-enchant technology itself.

In a time when AI is often framed as a threat, Kusano offers a different vision: one in which machines carry memory, care, and even spirit. Her images do not ask us to fear the future, but to imagine living within it — gently, imaginatively, and together.

Chapter 11: Phillip Toledano's — Another America

Phillip Toledano is a British-born, New York-based artist and photographer whose work has long blurred the boundaries between documentary, conceptual art, and personal narrative. Known for projects that explore identity, memory, and the cultural imagination, Toledano has shifted in recent years toward AI-generated imagery that reimagines history itself, positioning him as one of promptography's most thoughtful and provocative practitioners.

Reimagining the Past with AI

Toledano's project *Another America* uses generative AI to create a series of images set in the 1940s and 1950s — a period often remembered as the heyday of photography's *veracity*, when photographs were widely trusted as records of reality. He chose this era deliberately, because when you look at a photograph from the '40s or '50s — and because you've seen that kind of imagery before — you are already primed to assume it's true. By setting his project in a time before promptography existed, he could play with viewers' assumptions about truth, memory, and evidence.

The images in *Another America* range widely between the believable and the surreal: some look as if they could be historical photographs, while others clearly

50

could never have occurred — giant jellyfish clouds drifting over 1950s Manhattan, imagined disasters, strange events and invented characters that intertwine fact and fiction.

How He Works

Toledano's approach is rooted in his long experience with storytelling through images. In earlier photography-based projects like *The United States of Conspiracies*, he created elaborate staged works that referenced cultural narratives and political imagination. With *Another America*, he has found in AI the ability to build entire worlds digitally — including people, landscapes, "historical" events, and atmospheric details — without needing physical sets or subjects.

Working with AI is, in Toledano's words, both liberating and demanding. The generative systems he uses allow him to assemble complex scenes by writing and refining text prompts — essentially writing *descriptions* that then become images. This process requires thinking deeply about composition, characters, settings, era-specific details, the equivalent of camera angle and lens choice, and even the psychology of gesture and expression.

Toledano compares promptography to directing rather than photographing: instead of physically capturing light on film, he crafts and *directs* imagery from concept to execution. The analogy he uses is evocative: working with AI is like collaborating with "a very talented, very drunk person" — the system can produce something impressive quickly, but creating *nuanced, surreal, meaningful images* takes iteration, experimentation, and adjustment.

Examples from *Another America*

The *Another America* collection includes a striking array of AI-generated scenes, each rooted in a fictional version of mid-century America:

- "Giant Jellyfish Drifting Over" imagines massive jellyfish-like clouds over Manhattan caused by imagined industrial pollution — a scene that feels eerie and real yet could never have occurred, blending historical visual language with surreal invention.

- Other images show a crater in the middle of 1950s New York City, bizarre disasters, and whimsical objects like a child wearing a glass bubble on his head, deploying familiar photographic tropes while bending them into speculative visions.

These works deliberately span a spectrum from the plausible to the obviously impossible, inviting viewers to confront their own assumptions about photographic truth and historical imagery.

The Conceptual Stakes: Truth, Fiction, and History

At its core, *Another America* is not simply a creative exercise — it is a philosophical inquiry. Toledano's project questions how photography has long been held as a guarantor of truth, and what it means when AI can fabricate convincing evidence of events that never occurred. As he states, "With AI everything is true, and nothing is true" — and we now live in a moment where *every lie can have convincing visual evidence.*

This idea ties directly into the larger narrative of promptography. Where photography once offered *visual evidence of reality*, AI imagery blurs that line, generating visuals that feel historic even when they are fictional. Toledano suggests that we may be entering a time when the *visual truth* is no longer guaranteed — a world in which our relationship to images, memory, and belief must be fundamentally reconsidered.

Mixed Emotions About AI's Role

Toledano expresses both awe and ambivalence about AI. On one hand, AI enables unprecedented freedom in constructing imagined worlds: there are no boundaries! he says. On the other, he worries about the erosion of respect for careful photographic craft and the disappearance of the medium's historical weight. His reflections echo broader debates in visual culture about authenticity, representation, and the power of images in an age of AI.

And yet, like early photographers facing skepticism from painters in the 1850s, Toledano argues there *is* humanity — even soul — in AI-generated work. He suggests that objections based on a lack of "human touch" overlook the imaginative grounding and conceptual intention behind promptography.

What *Another America* Leaves Us With

Another America is more than an art project; it is a mirror held up to our visual culture. It asks us to reflect on how we understand history, how we interpret images, and how we adapt to a world where compelling visuals can be fabricated without ever capturing reality. In doing so, Toledano's work connects promptography not just to artistic experimentation, but to one of the central cultural questions of our time: What does it mean to believe what we see?

Chapter 12: Museums Reimagining the Past

For most of human history, images of lived experience simply didn't exist. Before the invention of the camera in the nineteenth century, there was no way to record reality directly with light. Painters, scribes, and illustrators documented people, places, and events—but always through interpretation, style, and varying levels of accuracy. So what does it mean when a museum today shows "photographs" of people from the seventeenth century? That question is becoming real in galleries around the world thanks to generative AI and promptography.

In 2024, Kalmar Museum in Sweden presented an exhibition titled *"Witches"* (*Häxor*) about the seventeenth-century witch trials. The modern camera did not exist during those events, yet visitors at the exhibition encountered portrait-like images of women, children, and judges connected to the history. These were not actual historical photographs, but AI-generated images produced by artist and exhibition producer Pompe Hedengren, who specifically used generative AI to imagine what people from that era might have looked like. The images were then integrated into the exhibition's narrative to help visitors connect more personally with the stories.

When the exhibition later traveled to Historiska Museet in Stockholm, it was noted as one of the first historical shows in Sweden to use AI to give faces to people who have never been photographed. In this context, generative imagery served to visualize human experience that would otherwise remain abstract and text-based.

Sweden's example is part of a broader trend. Museums internationally are exploring how AI-generated images and reinterpretations can complement traditional collections:

Around the world, some museums are experimenting with AI not just to display art but to re-imagine entire environments or timelines. The use of AI tools to generate imagined cities, reconstructions of lost architecture, or even speculative scenes of ancient life is increasingly part of digital heritage projects in Europe and North America—even if these efforts are still in early stages and often more conceptual than finalized.

Why Museums Use AI Imagery

Generative AI offers museums several potential benefits:

- **Making History More Personal**
AI imagery can give faces to anonymous historical actors who never had cameras trained on them, helping visitors connect emotionally with distant events. In *Häxor*, such images helped turn abstract names and dates into perceived individuals.

- **Filling Visual Gaps**
Where no visual record exists—such as earliest civilizations, remote cultures, or undocumented daily life—AI imagery can supplement exhibitions in ways traditional illustration cannot, generating visuals that feel historically grounded without claiming literal fact.

- **Engaging New Audiences**
Interactive visuals and AI interpretations often attract museumgoers who might otherwise find history inaccessible or text-heavy, broadening visitor engagement.

Risks and Ethical Considerations

At the same time, AI's ability to generate compelling, "photograph-like" images creates ethical challenges:

- **Authenticity vs. Imagination**
AI-generated images do *not* come from real visual evidence—they are statistical reconstructions based on modern datasets. This means they can be

convincing without being historically accurate, blurring the line between interpretation and documentation. Museums must carefully distinguish between *imagined representations* and real historical data so that audiences understand what they are seeing, not what it *looks* like.

• **Misinformation Potential**
When used outside museum contexts—on social media, blogs, or news sites—AI historical images can be mistaken for genuine archival material, contributing to confusion about historical fact. As some commentators have noted, images created without real sources can inadvertently fuel misinterpretations if not clearly labeled.

• **Cultural Sensitivity**
AI trained on biased or incomplete datasets reflects those limitations; using such systems to portray cultures, peoples, or events without context can unintentionally reinforce stereotypes or inaccuracies.

A Tool for Imagination — Not a Replacement for Evidence

Generative AI and promptography are transforming how museums think about presenting the past, especially for eras without cameras. They invite us to imagine what history might have looked like through a visual lens—but they do so by blending creativity and conjecture, not by unearthing forgotten snapshots of reality.

As museums continue experimenting with AI, the challenge will be to balance innovation with transparency: using AI as a tool to spark curiosity and connection, while always making clear that the images are interpretative reconstructions, not eyewitness records. In the world of cultural heritage, this new medium can open doors to engagement and empathy—but only if audiences understand its nature and limitations.

Chapter 13: Creating Your First Promptography

For many years, I have been interested in how artists use emerging technologies to create art—through the internet, video games, virtual and augmented reality, and, more recently, artificial intelligence. At heart, I am a writer, drawn to language and narrative, yet deeply fascinated by the visual world and its histories.

When DALL·E was released a few years ago, it opened an unexpected door. I began to combine my background in art history with my interest in language, using words as a tool to generate images. Text became image; writing became a way of seeing. Out of this process, several visual series emerged. One of them, *The Yolkers*, is a portrait series inspired by classical art-historical portraiture, depicting a fictional family whose heads are made of flowing egg yolk—simultaneously absurd, symbolic, and strangely intimate.

I also began experimenting with black-and-white photography generated through AI. One of these series, *Lights and Dreams*, gained international recognition in 2025 when it was awarded first prize in the 4th AI Arts Competition.

Lights and Dreams consists of monochrome images that borrow their aesthetic from early photographic art, capturing surreal, dreamlike scenes where light and darkness interact. In one image, a diver walks through the desert carrying a lit lantern in his hand. In another, an artist stands in moonlight inside a flooded studio, where the sea merges with the interior space and a painting within the image reflects the moon and the water beyond the walls. A third image shows an old, twisted tree in a storm, with a single candle flickering precariously on one of its branches.

These images do not depict real events; they depict imagined ones. They are photographs of fantasies—images that carry a narrative within them. They could just as easily serve as the opening scene of a film or a novel as stand alone as photographs.

There are many different strategies and philosophies for creating AI-generated images and promptographies. The field evolves rapidly: tools, models, and techniques change at a pace where what works one day may no longer work the next. Personally, I tend to keep my prompts relatively short and not overly specific. Rather than instructing the machine in detail, I try to describe the scene or image as I see it in my mind, drawing on my experience as a writer to choose words that evoke a particular mood, atmosphere, or emotional resonance.

As with most artistic processes, creating promptography is a matter of experimentation—of testing ideas, thinking freely, failing, adjusting, and trying again until something unexpected and meaningful emerges.

That said, there are also a number of fundamental principles, techniques, and practical approaches that can help guide the process. This chapter is an introduction to those tools and ways of thinking.

Promptography may seem mysterious at first: how can you write a photograph instead of taking one? The answer lies in understanding that your words become the camera, the lighting, and even the mood. When working with generative AI, your prompt is not just a description — it's a creative tool that shapes everything about the image.

This chapter will guide you through thinking like a promptographer, constructing prompts, using keywords, and refining your images to achieve the photographic effect you want.

1. Think Like a Photographer

Before you write your prompt, imagine yourself behind the camera. Consider these elements:

- **Subject:** Who or what is in the frame? A person, an object, a landscape, or a surreal hybrid?
- **Composition:** Close-up, wide angle, bird's-eye, or eye-level? How is the subject framed?
- **Lighting:** Soft natural light, dramatic studio lighting, neon glow, golden hour?
- **Style & Mood:** Documentary, cinematic, surreal, noir, vintage, dreamy?
- **Camera & Lens Effects:** Depth of field, bokeh, tilt-shift, fisheye, 50mm portrait lens, macro?

Writing a good prompt is like describing your ideal photo to a friend — the more vivid and detailed your description, the closer the AI can get to your vision.

2. Build Your Prompt Step by Step

A strong prompt usually contains **four layers**:

1. **Subject / Scene:** Who or what is in the image.
2. **Action / Environment:** What is happening and where.
3. **Stylistic Descriptors:** Mood, lighting, color, atmosphere, historical era.
4. **Technical / Camera Details:** Lens, angle, focus, film type, post-processing effect.

For example:

Prompt:
"A black-and-white portrait of a 1940s jazz musician playing saxophone on a rainy New York street, cinematic lighting, shallow depth of field, 50mm lens, grainy film texture, moody and atmospheric."

Notice how each component adds clarity to the AI. The subject (musician) + action/environment (playing in rainy street) + style/mood (cinematic, moody) + technical details (lens, grain) all work together.

3. Use Keywords for Photo Effects

Certain words or phrases consistently produce photographic qualities. Here are some categories and examples:

Lighting & Mood:

- Soft light, hard shadows, golden hour, neon glow, ambient light, chiaroscuro, dramatic lighting

Lens & Focus:

- Wide angle, telephoto, macro, fisheye, shallow depth of field, bokeh, focus on foreground/background

Texture & Film Quality:

- Grainy film, high contrast, Kodachrome, black and white, sepia, vintage, faded colors

Composition & Angle:

- Close-up, aerial view, eye-level, low-angle, centered, rule-of-thirds, symmetrical

Style & Genre:

- Documentary, surreal, cinematic, editorial, fashion photography, portrait, street photography, fine art

4. Think in Iterations

Rarely will a prompt produce your perfect image on the first try. Promptography is **iterative**:

- **Start simple:** Begin with your subject and setting.
- **Refine step by step:** Add lighting, mood, and style keywords.
- **Experiment:** Swap lens types, eras, or adjectives. "Noir" instead of "moody," "soft pastel" instead of "vibrant."
- **Analyze results:** What feels right? What is off? Adjust and rerun.

Remember: The AI interprets words differently than a human. Sometimes unexpected results produce beautiful accidents that become the heart of your promptography.

5. Combine Photography Knowledge with AI Creativity

Treat promptography like photography plus imagination:

- Knowledge of photography techniques helps you craft more precise prompts.
- Imagination lets you break rules, creating scenes that could never exist in reality.
- Consider era, culture, and lighting — these make AI-generated images more convincing.

For instance:
"A 1920s street scene in Tokyo, rainy night, neon reflections on wet pavement, cinematic black-and-white, 35mm lens, shallow focus, dramatic shadows"
This prompt leverages historical context, camera realism, and mood, producing a believable yet AI-generated scene.

6. Examples of Prompts

Example 1: Surreal Portrait
"A futuristic woman with glowing tattoos, sitting on a floating island, cinematic lighting, 85mm portrait lens, high detail, dramatic shadows, cyberpunk style."

Example 2: Historical Reconstruction
"A bustling 1950s Paris café scene, people drinking coffee, black-and-white photo, shallow depth of field, grainy film texture, moody atmosphere, eye-level shot."

Example 3: Abstract / Conceptual
"A giant clock melting over a city skyline at sunset, cinematic lighting, wide-angle lens, surreal photography style, high contrast, vibrant colors."

7. Ethical Considerations

Promptography is powerful, but with it comes responsibility:

- Clearly distinguish your AI-generated work from actual photography of real events.
- Avoid using AI to create misleading representations of people or history.
- Credit your AI tools if exhibiting or publishing work.

- Embrace the creative potential without claiming your images are "real" documentation.

8. Tools and Platforms

Some popular AI tools for promptography include:

- **MidJourney** – ideal for artistic and surreal styles.
- **DALL·E 3 / ChatGPT Image** – versatile, easy-to-refine prompts.
- **Stable Diffusion** – customizable, can run locally or online.
- **Runway / Leonardo AI** – combines editing and generation with video/animation options.

Most tools allow prompt refinement, negative prompts (telling the AI what to avoid), and seed adjustments for consistency.

9. Final Thoughts

Promptography is a blend of imagination, visual literacy, and language. The better you understand photography, the more effective your prompts. The more creative you are with language, the more surprising and unique your images will become.

Start small. Observe. Iterate. And remember: every "happy accident" generated by AI is a step toward your own unique visual language.

Promptography is not just about making images—it's about learning to see, think, and write like a photographer, even without a camera.

www.ingramcontent.com/pod-product-compliance
Lightning Source LLC
Chambersburg PA
CBHW050017230526
45470CB00003B/1007